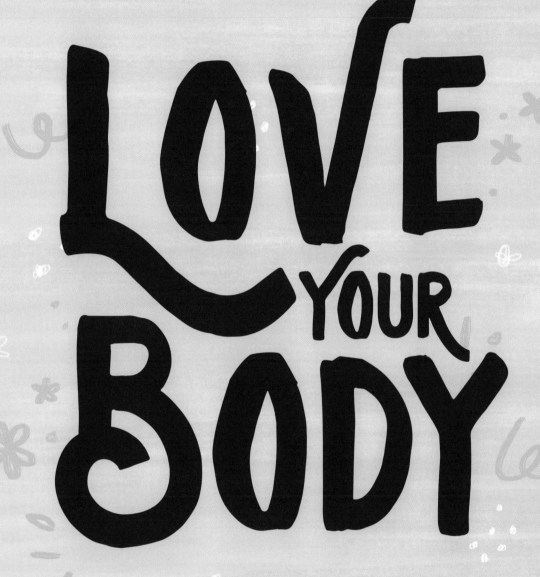

LOVE YOUR BODY

by Jessica Sanders
illustrated by Carol Rossetti

FIVE
MILE

For Sophie,

your legacy lives on in our hearts
and through our actions.

J.S.

FIVE MILE

Five Mile, the publishing division of Regency Media
Suite 148, 425 Smith Street, Fitzroy VIC 3065, Australia
www.fivemile.com.au

First published 2019

Written by Jessica Sanders
Illustrations by Carol Rossetti
Text copyright © Jessica Sanders 2019
Illustration copyright © Jessica Sanders 2019
Visit: www.re-shape.info

Jessica Sanders asserts her right to be identified as the author of this work.
Carol Rossetti asserts her right to be identified as the illustrator of this work.
Designed by Stephanie Spartels, Studio Spartels.
Illustrator's photo on page 40: copyright © Carolina Vianna, 2019 and used with permission.

ISBN: 978-1-76068-489-1

Printed in China 5 4 3 2 1

NOTE TO THE READER

To the girls,

It is my hope that this book will **comfort** you,
guide you and **empower** you. I want you to know
that you are **extraordinary** exactly as you are.
Once you know this to be true nothing will be able
to hold you back — you and your **incredible** body
will be able to do anything, so dream big.

Your friend,
Jess

AUTHOR'S NOTE

This book has been written for girls and those who identify as a girl. However, the language I have used is not gendered and the overarching message is universal. Negative body image can affect anyone, regardless of gender, race or sexual orientation. This book draws on my postgraduate studies in gender and social work as well as my own experiences as a girl and young woman struggling with society's unrealistic expectations of 'beauty'. The messages in this book have also been influenced by a body functionality approach, feminist theory and the body positive movement.

Love Your Body has been created to be understood by a range of readers. Children younger than the recommended reading age of 8+ should be able to navigate the book with the support of a parent, carer or teacher. Even if a child is not able to understand all of the language, they should understand the visual messages. The illustrations send a strong, clear message and it is important that young girls be exposed to this message as early as possible.

Your body is **unique**.

No one has a body quite like yours and that's amazing!

Every body is **different**
and **EVERY** body is a good body.

Your body is always changing and you
will notice some of the biggest changes
when you go through puberty*.

*Puberty is a time when your
body changes and grows on
the inside and outside to look
more like an adult's body.

Going through puberty can feel like a **weird time.**
Your body will change on the **inside** and the **outside.**
Your body will become bigger and it will take up
more space, and **that's okay!**

Bodies come in all different **forms** and **abilities.** All these bodies are different and all these bodies are good bodies.

There is no one **size**, ability or **colour** that is perfect. What makes you different makes you, you — and you are **amazing!**

It's important to **accept** and **love**
yourself exactly as you are.
Do not wait until tomorrow,
start right now.

Our bodies are **amazing!**

They can do so many **incredible** things.

Bodies are not just to be looked at
and admired — our bodies are
so much more than that.

If you are ever finding it hard to love your body, try writing a list of all the great things that your body helps you to do.

Here are some examples.

I love that my ears can hear music and that my body can dance to the sound.

I love that my body is strong enough to pick up my little brother and give him a big cuddle.

I love that my
hands help me to create
beautiful things.

I love that my eyes can see
my favourite TV show and
read my favourite book.

I love that my nose
can smell the saltiness of
the sea and the flowers
in the garden.

If that list isn't working, here is another list of helpful things you can do when you're feeling a little down. Taking time to look after your mind and body is called 'self-care'. Self-care is a great way of showing kindness to yourself and it's a skill you can use throughout your whole life.

1

Stand in front of the mirror and say, "MY BODY IS STRONG. MY BODY CAN DO AMAZING THINGS. MY BODY IS MY OWN."

2

Go outside and connect with nature. Find a nice tree to sit under, or lie on some grass and feel the blades of grass on your skin.

3

Write down three things you are truly grateful for.

4

Put on a crazy and colourful outfit and strut around acting confident until you actually start feeling that way!

5

Put on your favourite tunes REALLY LOUD and dance crazily just for you! You will find a smile creeping onto your face. You won't be able to stop it.

7

Learn how to knit, crochet, cross-stitch or draw mandalas. It's really calming to use your hands and concentrate on one thing.

6

Help a friend or family member. It can be a relief to get out of your own head and help others. It will make you feel really good to do something for someone else.

9

Try taking photos of things around your house. Looking at life through a camera lens can help you see things differently, and it's a great way to be creative.

8

Do some slow stretching in a quiet place; this will help you feel more at home in your body. If you want to, you could try doing some yoga. There are lots of free videos online to help you get started.

10

Search for positive quotes until you find one that has meaning for you. Print it out or write it down, and keep it with you. Look at it when you're feeling down.

If you ever try some of these things and they aren't making you feel better, then it's very important you seek help from a trusted adult or from one of the organisations listed in the back of this book.

Everyone needs to ask for help
sometimes — you are **not alone.**

Your body really is quite incredible, and
if you listen you can hear it speaking to you.
Your body will tell you what it needs by
sending signals — it's really smart like that!
Your body will let you know when you need to eat,
and it will let you know when you need to rest.

Listening to your body and giving
it what it needs is another way that
you can practise self-care.